# HEATHROW

**The world's busiest international airport**

# HEATHROW

## The world's busiest international airport

**Mike Jerram**

OSPREY
AEROSPACE

# Acknowledgements

Thanks are due to a number of people at Heathrow Airport without whom few of the photographs in this book could have been taken. Special thanks go to Brian Salter, indefatigable 'can do' Public Affairs Manager for Heathrow Airport Limited, whose intimate knowledge of the airport's complex geography ensured access to parts that even dedicated lager drinkers couldn't, and for his companionship and service beyond the call of duty in the hot summer of 1990 when only *winter-weight* versions of the airside-mandatory high-viz jackets were available. And for their help in easing me into the busy routines of their airlines, appreciation to Peter Baldry and Malcolm Wadman of Air Canada, Jim Vick and Ian Busby of British Airways, Mark Olney of Cathay Pacific, Oliver Evans of KLM Royal Dutch Airlines, Terry Whitby of Singapore Airlines (the chilled orange juice you brought from MegaTop's galley in the 100°F swelter of the flight deck tasted like a life saver), to the many bemused cockpit crews who must have wondered what that camera-festooned character was doing lurking around taxiways or under the approach lights, and to those cheery passengers who gave a wave as they taxied by at the start or end of their journeys. And finally, thanks to Editor Dennis 'mine's a pint' Baldry for his long-haul effort in getting this book accelerated up to $V_r$ and away, and for his photographic contributions when he had to force himself (!) away from the editorial 'flight deck' to get behind the viewfinder.

The photographs in this book were shot with Nikon cameras and lenses, on Kodachrome 25, Fujichrome Velvia and Fujichrome 100 25 film.

Published in 1991 by Osprey Publishing Limited
59 Grosvenor Street, London W1X 9DA

© Mike Jerram

British Library Cataloguing in Publication Data

Jerram, Mike
    Heathrow: the world's busiest international airport.
    1. Heathrow airport
    I. Title
    387.7360942183

ISBN 0 85045 766 1

Editor Dennis Baldry
Page design David Tarbutt
Printed in Hong Kong

For a catalogue of all books published by Osprey Aerospace please write to:

**The Marketing Department,
Octopus Illustrated Books, 1st Floor, Michelin House,
81 Fulham Road, London SW3 6RB**

**Front cover** Heathrow is the only airport in the UK where you'll see scheduled Concorde operations. Snoot drooped, this British Airways' 'Speedbird' makes a typically dramatic tyre-smoking arrival

**Title page** Watched by a crowd of spectators on the viewing gallery, an Alitalia Douglas DC-9 departs from the Foxtrot stands of Terminal 2 against a backdrop of Heathrow's most famous landmark, its brick-built control tower

**Back cover** Hustle at Heathrow: an Olympic Airways Airbus A300 taxies out as a British Airways Boeing 757 climbs away in the background

The first long-haulers. This memorial to pioneering aviators Captain John Alcock and Lieutenant Arthur Whitten Brown was unveiled on 15 June 1954, the 35th anniversary of the first nonstop transatlantic flight. Since moved to its present location in the central area, it has seen the departure and arrival of who knows how many thousands of Atlantic crossings in the wake of their Vickers Vimy

# Introduction

Seventy-two years ago the first international flight from London bumped aloft from Hounslow Heath, heading for Paris. Today jet airliners arriving at England's capital fly over the site of that first departure every 90 seconds, inbound to London-Heathrow.

Around 2000 BC 'Hetherewe' was home to a neolithic tribe (the site is thought to be at a point about 300 yards along Runway 27R). In the eighteenth century it was an area renowned for highway robbery (no jokes, please), but it was not until 1929 that aircraft manufacturer Sir Richard Fairey established the Great West Aerodrome which was later requisitioned under war emergency powers to make way for 'a new Royal Air Force station', in reality a thinly-disguised government plan to turn it into a post-war 'super airport'.

And so it is. From its beginnings in 1946 as London Airport—ever-beloved by small boy aircraft spotters as 'LAP'—when the 'terminal buildings' consisted of army-surplus brown canvas tents, duckboards, elsan toilets and oil heaters, Heathrow has grown to become the world's busiest international airport, handling more than 42 million passengers a year and up to 1200 aircraft movements per day on its two parallel runways, which are used simultaneously for take-offs and landings. LHR has a workforce of more than 53,000 people—equivalent to the population of a large town; 57 million items of baggage are handled at the airport annually, and there are 9200 trolleys on which to push them. The fuel farm, linked directly to refineries via underground pipelines, pumps more than three billion litres of Jet A1 each year; and for fuelling passengers, the airport's restaurants and cafeterias serve 23,500 cups of tea, 6500 pints of beer and 11,500 sandwiches each day.

While Chicago O'Hare and several other US airports may handle more traffic overall, London-Heathrow is the unrivalled king of international air transport, truly the Crossroads of the World.

# Contents

Little and large. The two extremes of British Airways' Heathrow-based fleet: Boeing 737-200 *River Ouse* and the appropriately named 747-400 *City of London*, briefly running neck-and-neck on inner and outer taxiways

# Long Haul

The final mile. British Airways Boeing 747 Flight BA018 slides down the 27R glideslope after a flight from Tokyo-Narita via Moscow-Sheremetyevo

Latest version of the ubiquitous Jumbo is the 747-400, readily distinguishable by its six-foot high winglets, claimed to offer a three per cent increase in range through enhanced aerodynamic efficiency and drag reduction. The -400 also has a 12-foot increase in span over earlier 747s and adopts a notably droop-winged appearance on the ground. BA's 747-436s are powered by Rolls-Royce RB211-524G turbofans, each rated at 58,000 lb st. Ranges of 7000 + nautical miles are attainable by the 747-400. One operated by Qantas Airways set a world distance

record in 1989 flying non-stop from Heathrow to Sydney, a distance of 9688 nm, while on its delivery flight to the Australian carrier

**Left** Way to go! Riding the combined 152,000 lb st thrust of its four reheated Rolls-Royce/SNECMA Olympus 593-610 turbojets, Concorde BA001 lifts off from Runway 09R bound for New York, just over three hours away. Take-off would have been at about 215 knots, pitch angle increasing to maintain 250 knots until cleared by ATC to begin accelerating to subsonic climb speed of Mach 0.95 and going supersonic after clearing the south coast of Wales. Mach 2 (a mile every 2.75 seconds) is achieved around the time cabin crew serve lunch. Ho, hum … Faster than the sun? Well, in a way. On winter schedules you can depart Heathrow after dusk on the evening Concorde flight to JFK and watch the sun 'rise' out of the west (*Dennis Baldry*)

**Overleaf** British Airways' long-haul flights, including Concorde, all use Heathrow's Terminal 4. Pictured here are two Boeing 747-246s, a 747-436 and a Lockheed TriStar. Opened in April 1986, Terminal 4 caters for eight million passengers a year and is situated on the airport's south side, overlooking Runway 09R/27L. Distinctive features of Terminal 4 are its completely segregated arrivals and departures areas and its single departure lounge, as big as three football pitches

**Preceding pages** Clippers *Gem of the Ocean* and *Pride of the Sea* display old and new Pan American liveries. Stand marker board framing *Gem of the Ocean* is a sighting device enabling aircraft captains to stop their aircraft with the forward cabin door precisely aligned with the telescopic airbridge

**These pages and overleaf** Singapore Airlines call their new 747-412s 'MegaTops' (their -312s are 'Big Tops'). First Class, in the forward fuselage section, and Business Class in the extended upper deck, offer sumptuous comforts for the 13–14 hour non-stop trip between Heathrow and Singapore's Changi Airport. Dash 400 Jumbos have fully digital 'all glass' EFIS-equipped cockpits and are configured for two-pilot operation. Pilots can sleep in bunks situated behind the flight deck while a second pair takes over en route, but legal requirements mean that the crew performing the take-off must also be in command for the landing

Weeks after *Shat-Al-Arab* operated this flight from Baghdad, Iraq annexed Kuwait and Iraqi Airways Boeing 747s were banned from Heathrow. But one of the Iraqi flag carrier's 747s returned to Heathrow in December 1990 to assist in the repatriation of British hostages freed by President Saddam Hussein

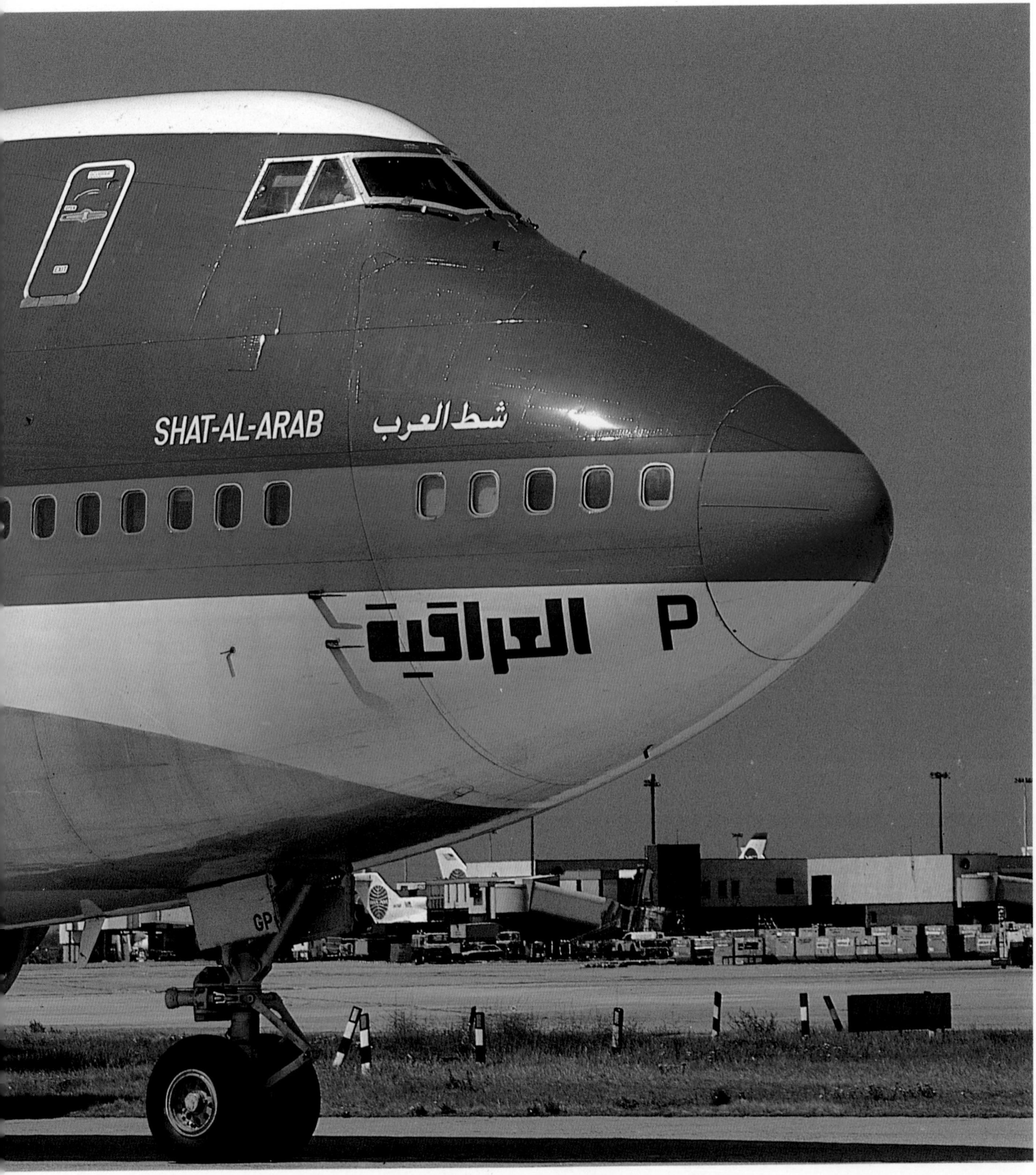

SHAT-AL-ARAB
شط العرب
العراقية
P
GP

*Shat-Al-Arab*, one of Iraqi Airways' small fleet of 747-200Cs, rotates as it begins the return flight to Saddam International Airport, Baghdad. The Gulf crisis eliminated the hard-won economic gains made by the carrier, which would have otherwise returned to profitability

**Following three spreads** Air Canada Flight AC888, a TriStar from Toronto, rolls up to a remote stand and within seconds is surrounded by mobile airstairs, hi-lift container loaders, toilet emptying 'honey carts' and the ubiquitous yellow buses of Whytes Airport Services to take passengers to Terminal 3. Meanwhile in the cockpit AC888's flight crew Captains Carl Jadeski, Sandy Merrithew and Flight Engineer Jim Thwaites shut down systems and square away paperwork before disembarking after a pleasant, routine transatlantic trip with no problems save for a few easily avoided storms

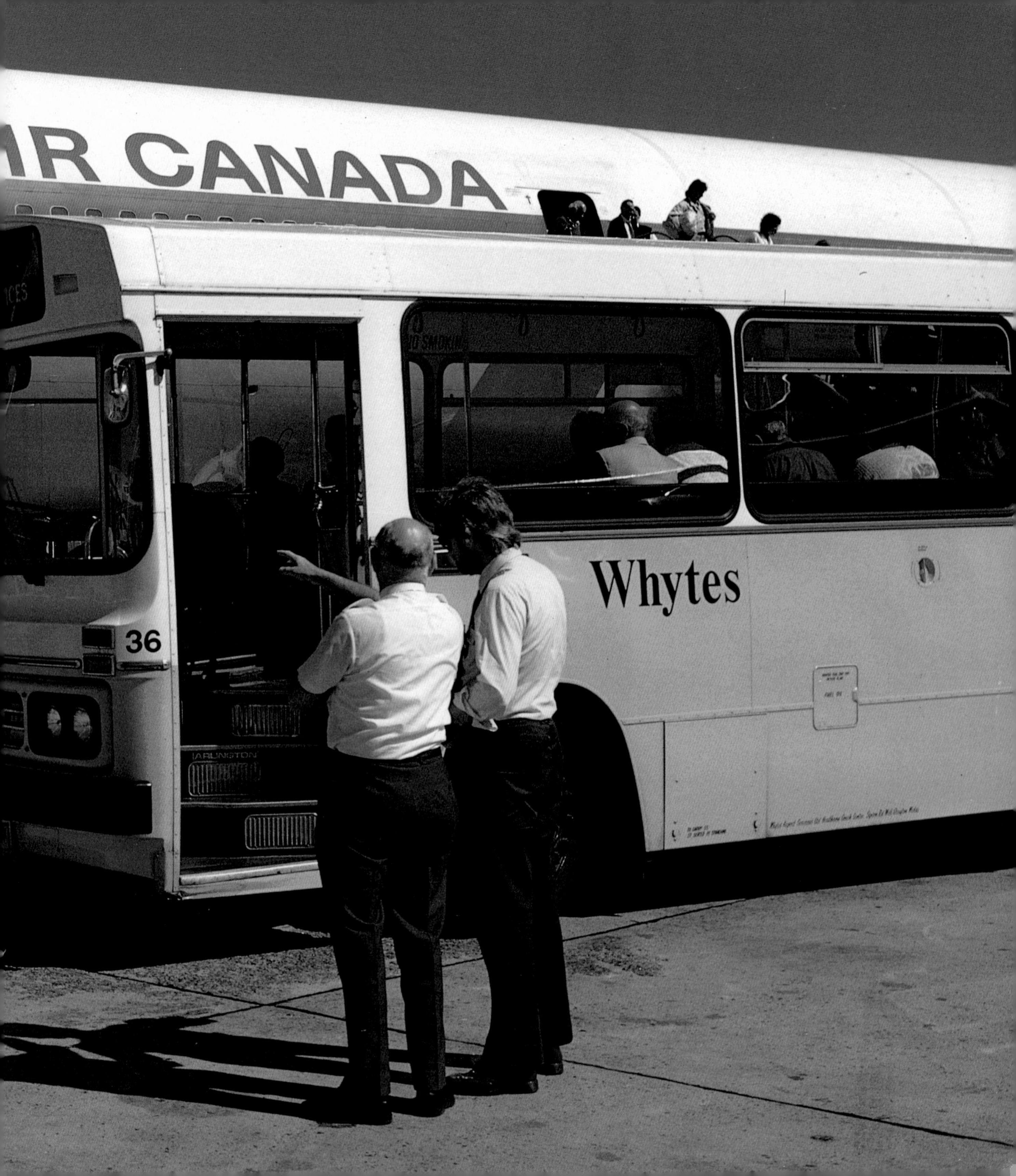
IR CANADA
Whytes
36

So reliable have the new generation civilian turbofan engines proved that in 1987 the Federal Aviation Administration granted approval for extended range operations (EROPS) by Boeing 767s, paving the way for these and other large twin-engine airliners to operate routes involving lengthy flights over water or undeveloped land areas that previously would have required three- or four-engined aircraft. This Trans World Airlines 767-231ER is taxying for a flight to Philadelphia, while its three-engined TriStar stablemate is Boston-bound

**Overleaf** British Airways has ordered 15 Boeing 767-300s, powered by Rolls-Royce RB211-524H engines, and introduced the type into service during the summer of 1990

**Preceding pages** Still bearing a French overseas registration, one of six Airbus A310-304s to bear the distinctive charcoal grey and gold markings of Royal Jordanian Airlines. The A310's crowned fin is an all-composite structure

Middle East 707s: a plushly-outfitted government-owned example from Qatar, and a workaday but immaculate cargo mover from Middle East Airlines

# Short/Medium Haul

**Above** Austrian Airlines' MD-81 *Niederosterreich*, newly arrived from Vienna

**Right** Scandinavian Airlines System McDonnell Douglas MD-81 *Torkel Viking* arriving from Copenhagen. First of the MD developments of the Douglas DC-9, the MD-81 seats up to 172 passengers and is powered by two Pratt & Whitney JT8D-209 turbofans

**Following spread** Tails from Europe. Boeing 737-230 of Lufthansa, MD-81s of Austrian Airlines and Swissair and DC-9-32 of Alitalia

**Below and overleaf** Lufthansa Boeing 737–330 *Reutlingen* on the inner taxiway bound for Terminal 2's cul-de-sacs after operating Flight LH1656 from Munich. Note larger, flat-bottomed nacelles of the 737-300 series' CFM56 turbofans compared to those of the earlier Pratt & Whitney JT8Ds on British Airways 737–236 *River Derwent* (pictured right)

Spanish carrier Viva Air operates a fleet of five Boeing 737-300s, and has a nice line in modern art colour schemes. EC-ELY is seen here on arrival from Palma, and exactly one hour later, pushed back and ready to return with another load of sun-seeking holidaymakers. The ground engineer is making final checks with the flight deck crew before disconnecting his communications 'wander lead', which he will hold aloft to show that he is safely clear and the aircraft free to taxi

**Left** Precisely tracking the yellow guideline, Alitalia Douglas DC-9-32 *Isola di Murano* noses in to Terminal 2's stand Foxtrot 2 after arriving from Milan-Linate

**Below left** British Midland's 'Diamond Service' fleet of DC-9s are all named after famous gems. Here DC-9-30 *The Regent Diamond* gets airborne from 27L on the afternoon service to Dublin

**Below** British Aerospace ATPs are used on British Midland's services to London from its base at East Midlands Airport

**Overleaf** Tug disconnected, ground handler coiling his intercom lead, Iberia's Flight IB615 is ready for departure to Valencia

Berlin-Tegel bound passengers board
*Clipper Endeavour,* a Boeing 727-235
operating Pan American Flight
PA102

**Below** British Airways inherited a fleet of ten undelivered Airbus A320-111s when it took over British Caledonian. *Isle of Anglesey* G-BUSI is seen arriving from Frankfurt

**Right** Once the workhorse of European airlines, Sud Caravelles are seldom seen at Heathrow nowadays. Aero France International's F-GEPC arrived from Paris-Le Bourget

**Below right** Caught in the afterglow, a Boeing 727-230 operating Lufthansa Flight LH1604, arrives from Frankfurt/Main

**These pages and overleaf** Eastern Bloc. Inbound from Warsaw and Budapest, Tupolevs Tu-154M of *Polskie Linie Lotnicze* (LOT) and Tu-154B of Hungarian carrier Malev, while another Tu-154B of Balkan Bulgarian tucks up its gear en route for Sofia

British Airways' Boeing 757-236 *Conway Castle* pushes back for a mid-morning Shuttle service to Edinburgh … while another of BA's hard-working 757 fleet makes an early evening arrival from Zurich

**Next three spreads** Airbuses all. On short finals, Swissair A310-221 *Basel-Land* inbound from Geneva. Olympic Airways' A300B4 *Achilleus* amid the frantic bustle of a rapid turnaround, with catering trucks, toilet service units, baggage lorries, fresh water tankers and container loaders all in attendance in preparation for the twice-daily service to Athens. Burning rubber, Air Portugal A310-304 touches down on 27L after a flight from Lisbon. Cyprus Airways A310-203 taxies for a 27L departure for Larnaca, while Lufthansa A300-603 *Bingen* gets away to Frankfurt/Main. Turkish Airlines' A310-203 *Aras* arriving from Istanbul, while an Airport Fire Service Gloster Saro Javelin foam tender speeds by en route to a remote area of the airport for a practice fire drill

# Airport Aspects

Night falls on Heathrow's central area, dominated by the control tower. From the green-tinted, double-glazed windows of the visual control room (VCR) Arrivals Controllers handle all aerial movements after handover from the approach controllers who monitor radar screens in darkness eight floors below, while Air Departures Controllers see flights safely airborne before handover to controllers at the London Air Traffic Control Centre at nearby West Drayton. Ground Movement Controllers orchestrate aircraft, vehicles, and *anything* that moves on the runways, taxiways and ramp areas, aided in bad visibility or at night by the Airfield Surface Movement Indicator, whose radar scanner tops off the 120-foot high tower

Each year 13 million vehicles use Heathrow's Main Tunnel, which links the M4 and A4 roads with the central area and travels under Runway 09L/27R. The airport has over 40 miles of its own roads. In this view British Airways' Boeing 757s can be seen manoeuvring on the taxiways leading to Terminal 1's stands, while a LOT Tupolev Tu-154 lands on 27R. The billboard at the tunnel's mouth and the 'triangle' at the entry/exit point divide are prime advertising sites, the latter being used here to launch Rover Cars' new Metro range (*Dennis Baldry*)

Terminal 1, opened in November 1968, is the busiest of the airport's four terminals, handling more than 17 million passengers each year, 60 per cent of them travelling on business. The volume of traffic handled by this terminal alone would make it Europe's sixth busiest 'airport' in its own right. British Airways operates its domestic and most of its European flights from here. Other tenant airlines include Aer Lingus, Air UK, British Midland, Brymon Airways, Cyprus Airways, Dan Air, El Al, Icelandair, Manx, Sabena and South African Airways. T1 has independent road systems serving departures and arrivals. A proposed high speed rail link will bring passengers from London's Paddington Station right into Terminal 1 in 16 minutes (*Dennis Baldry*)

**Left** Terminal 2 was the first passenger terminal to be built in Heathrow's central area, opening as 'The Europa Building' in 1955. It, and the Queens Building, were inaugurated on 16 December of that year by Her Majesty the Queen. T2 is used by more than 20 European airlines and each year handles over eight million passengers flying to 90 destinations. The spectators' area on the roof of Terminal 2 provides a fine view of operations from Runways 09R/27L and the less-frequently used 05/23, beyond which can be seen British Airways' extensive maintenance bases, and is popular with aircraft spotters, daytrippers and wellwishers waving off or greeting passengers. Some 30,000 'meeters and greeters' and 2000 spectators visit Heathrow each day (*Dennis Baldry*)

**Below** A colourful Ghana Airways Douglas DC-10 is parked on a remote stand adjacent to Terminal 3, from which a Trans World Airlines Lockheed L-1011 TriStar takes the outer taxiway for departure from 27L. Beyond the runway can be seen the VIP Suite (immediately above the L-1011's fin) and the cargo terminal with nightstopping Gulfstream bizjet and Nigerian Airways Boeing 707 in attendance (*Dennis Baldry*)

This control room in D'Albiac House, near Terminal 1, is the nerve centre of BAA's Apron Control Unit. Here the mind-boggling jigsaw of stand allocations and handling requirements is juggled. The airport has 163 parking stands with up to 80 aircraft landing or taking off hourly at busiest periods. The ACU has to make sure all aircraft have stands allocated of the right size at the correct terminal at the right time, and is also responsible for updating a computerized flight information system which makes operational data available to other users throughout the airport

Once the pride of British Overseas Airways Corporation's fleet, de Havilland Comet IV G-APDT ended its days providing practice for Heathrow's fire and rescue services, and became such a landmark that its grassy resting place at the western end of the apron was referred to as 'Comet Corner' by ground controllers passing instructions to taxying airliners. A few days after this picture was taken 'DT became the last Comet to leave Heathrow—on breakers' trucks—and was replaced by an ex-British Airways Trident (*Dennis Baldry*)

Ecological paradox though it may be, birds love airports and aren't in the least bothered by aircraft noise or kerosene fumes, so birdstrikes are an ever present risk. At Heathrow the counter-threat is provided by *Seagull Patrol* from HAL's Manoeuvring Area Safety Unit (MASU), whose Land Rover is equipped with a Digiscare amplified sound system

that can play the warning cries of the most common species to be found at the airport—lapwings, gulls, rooks and starlings. The effect is shortlived, and doesn't disturb the smaller bird varieties, so John Kirkham tries a shell cracker round, making sure that sight of a pistol and sound of the shot are out of range of anyone who might misinterpret his intentions. *Seagull Patrol*, here made up of Kirkham and colleague Mike Niemynski, and their counterparts in *Checker*, also patrol runways, taxiways and ramp areas, checking the thousands of guidance lights and watching for surface damage or debris that could cause catastrophic FOD (foreign object damage)

You can see a P-51 any day at Heathrow. Displayed in the roof garden above the Queen's Building is this model of *Excalibur III*, the P-51C Mustang which American Captain Charles F 'Chuck' Blair flew non-stop from New York's Idlewild Airport (now JFK International) to London Airport, as it was then known, on 31 January 1951 in a record time of 7 hours 48 minutes for an average speed of 442 mph. Blair later founded the Antilles Air Boats airline in the Caribbean, and died in the crash of a Grumman Goose amphibian. The Mustang was donated in his memory by his widow, Hollywood star Maureen O' Hara. The full-size *Excalibur III* is preserved in the National Air & Space Museum, Washington, DC

**Left** The mountains of waste paper that blow across Heathrow's acres are tackled by low-tech but effective spike sticks and plastic bin bags

**Above** Always using the callsign *Kittiwake*, aircraft of The Queen's Flight are frequent visitors to Heathrow's plush high-security Royal VIP Suite located well away from prying eyes on the south side near the cargo terminal. On this day Andover CC. 1 XS790's VIP passenger was the Duchess of Kent

# Maintenance

**Opposite page** Concorde's distinctive ogival delta planform silhouetted through the doors of British Airways' SST engineering base at Cranebank, where the aircraft was undergoing routine checks before operating the afternoon service to New York. Unfortunately removed before the picture was taken was a dartboard, positioned by BA engineers so that Concorde's nose-mounted pitot probe scored a perfect bullseye!

**Right and preceding page** All Concorde maintenance is performed at Cranebank, on the eastern side of Heathrow. Just one part of BA's massive engineering facilities at the airport, aircraft must be towed across a public road to reach it by way of the world's largest pair of level crossing gates

If you don't work at Cranebank, the best way to get an engineer's eye view of a Concorde is to visit the Imperial War Museum at Duxford in Cambridgeshire or the Fleet Air Arm Museum at Yeovilton in Somerset, where the prototype 002 G-BSST and the pre-production 01 G-AXDN are respectively preserved. Only 20 Concordes were built; British Airways and Air France each received seven production aircraft

**Below** The appropriately registered G-HUGE awaiting a tug to return to service after paintwork. Overhead gantries and custom-built staging are essential for servicing these behemoths

# Bizjets

**Left** First flown in 1957 to meet a USAF requirement for a utility transport and trainer, the Lockheed JetStar was among the first dedicated business jets on the market, and unusual in having four engines—3700 lb st Garrett TFE 731-3 turbofans in the case of this JetStar II

**Above** Field's Executive Jet Centre provides FBO services for many of the corporate aircraft visiting Heathrow, and a home for several London-based fleets of executive jets. Gulfstreams predominate. This one is a Gulfstream II retrofitted with the wingletted wing of the Gulfstream III, to make it a G-IIB, and is operated by the Atlantic Richfield petroleum company

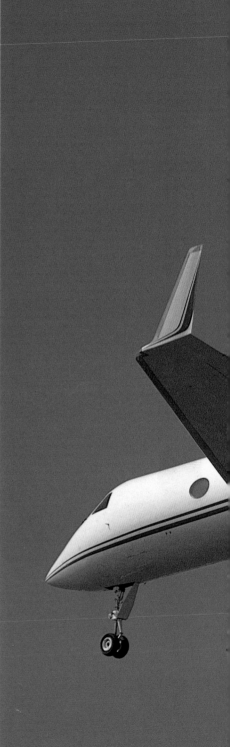

**Above** Not surprisingly, offshore financial havens boast substantial numbers of business jets on their civil aircraft registers. This pair of Gulfstreams are Cayman Islands-registered. G-III VR-CCN awaits its passengers in the cargo area, while Jet Fly Aviation's VR-CYM, readily identifiable as a G-IV by its longer cabin and large nacelles housing Rolls-Royce Tay 610-8 turbofans, rotates from Runway 27L bound for ... who knows where? Discretion and security go hand-in-hand in bizjet operations

**Right** A visitor from the East. Site Corporation's Saudi Arabian-registered Gulfstream III inbound to 27R

**Overleaf** The British Aerospace 125 is one of the world's sucessful medium-size business jets, and always well to the fore on the Field's ramp. Here Dravidian Air Services' locally-based Model 700B (foreground) is seen in company with a German-owned example and a Royal Air Force BAe 125 CC.2 from No 32 Sqn, the VIP transport unit based at nearby RAF Northolt. The CC.2 is a BAe 125–600, but in deference to Northolt's neighbours (and the high-ranking government ministers for whom it is a runabout) its noisy and thirsty Armstrong Siddeley Viper turbojets have been replaced by the quiet, fuel-efficient Garret TFE731 turbofans of later model 125-700/800s

**Below left** Heavy metal. The tasteful grey pinstripe of Hemmeter Aviation's corporate Boeing 727-35 is highlighted by the golden rays of dawn after overnighting on Heathrow's cargo ramp

**Left and below** Gulfstream gathering: Occidental Petroleum Corporation's G-IV N2OXY, one of several business jets used by its celebrated Chairman Dr Armand Hammer, all with OXY N-number suffixes; General Electric Capital Corporation's G-III; and Paramount Communications' G-IIB

# Cargo

Heathrow's World Cargocentre
covers an area of 160 acres. It has 25
aircraft stands and anually handles
more than 650,000 tonnes of cargo
valued at over £30 billion. This
represents 15.8 per cent of all visible
trade through British ports, and 76
per cent through all British airports.
The Cargocentre has its own road
system, access tunnel to the central
area, hydrant refuelling for aircraft
and nearly 100,000 square metres of
bonded transit shed space. Its ACP90
computerized inventory system is the
most sophisticated in the world,
enabling a cargo consignment to be
tracked through every stage of its
journey

**Above and overleaf** Heathrow's rising sun has barely risen as Japan Air Lines cargo flight JL623, a Boeing 747-246F, arrives at the Cargocentre from Tokyo-Narita via Anchorage, Alaska

**This page and bottom right** The world's ten biggest cargo carriers produced a total of 30.9 billion revenue tonne-kilometres in 1989; Japan Air Lines is number three in the air cargo league table behind the clear market leader, Federal Express, and Lufthansa

**Left** New and replacement engines for Heathrow-based operators are regular freight

The venerable Seven-Oh still serves
with a number of cargo operators.
This is one of three 707-3F9Cs flying
with Nigeria Airways

**Preceding pages and this page**
0430. Cathay Pacific Boeing 747-267F arrived less than an hour ago from Hong Kong via Dubai and is already being loaded with a return cargo, which includes race horses. The 747-200F series can carry up to 250,000 lb of cargo, 200,000 lb of it containerized or palletized on the main deck. Thanks to built-in handling systems and self-propelled cargo loaders that enable two men to load the aircraft to capacity in 30 minutes, CX038 will be away again at 0655, back to HKG via Paris-Charles de Gaulle

Long retired from passenger service in Europe, where it was operated by KLM, the Lockheed L-188 Electra is making a comeback as a stalwart of the overnight package carrying business. This one is operated by East Midlands-based Air Bridge Carriers for EMS International Post Corporation

Palletized loads going aboard an Air Canada Boeing 747-238B Combi, whose passenger/cargo configuration permits up to 12 main deck pallets/containers to be carried in the rear section, separated from the forward passenger compartments by a bulkhead. Until the human cargo goes aboard, a tailstand is necessary to maintain an even keel

Iran Air flight IR4702, a Boeing 747-200F, on the outer taxiway to 27R for an afternoon flight to the Iranian capital, Teheran

**Below and overleaf** Prior to the Gulf crisis Iraqi Airways Ilyushin Il-76MD *Candid Bs* were frequent visitors to the Cargocentre, but photography of the aircraft and their loads was not welcomed either by their crews or the large posse of police and customs officials which attended each arrival. Iraqi Airways has a fleet of more than 30 Il-76s, which are operated on behalf of the military services

FedEx it. McDonnell Douglas DC-10-30CF N301FE bears the unmistakable purple and orange of cargo giant Federal Express, while Boeing 747-245F N640FE *Houston Rehrig* is more discreetly labelled and still bears the largely unpainted livery of the celebrated Flying Tigers, now part of the FedEx empire

**Last page** TriStar at sunset